The Craft of Writing

O. M. Thomson

Oxford University Press 1981

Oxford University Press, Walton Street, Oxford OX2 6DP

Oxford   London   Glasgow
New York   Toronto   Melbourne   Wellington
Kuala Lumpur   Singapore   Hong Kong   Tokyo
Delhi   Bombay   Calcutta   Madras   Karachi
Nairobi   Dar es Salaam   Cape Town

ISBN 0 19 831244 X

© O. M. Thomson 1981

Photoset in Great Britain by
Rowland Phototypesetting Ltd
Bury St Edmunds, Suffolk
and printed by Spottiswoode Ballantyne Ltd
Colchester, Essex

To the student

In this book we study some of the different ways in which people write—Somerset Maugham's way, for example, or Graham Greene's, or Ian Fleming's, or Barbara Cartland's, or the way a popular journalist writes, or an advertisement copy-writer, or a university professor.

The aim is to help you to improve your technique and style. So your attention will be drawn only to certain aspects of these different ways of writing. 'Will it help you to improve,' I asked myself, 'if I explain this point or that point?' Only if I thought it would, did I include it.

Each lesson takes up two pages. On the left hand page we look at a certain way of writing, and we draw some conclusions about it; and on the right hand page you are given written exercises to do, in which you can test these conclusions for yourself.

Contents

Sentences

Words

Punctuation

Imagery

Presenting an argument

Sentences

1 Clear sentences

If something is well written the reader will be able to give his whole attention to what the writer is saying. But he will not be able to if it is badly written, because then some of his attention will be taken up with sorting out the muddle. A good writer sorts out his own muddles. He considers his readers. He remembers that they are giving him their attention, and he is careful not to waste any of it.

Here is a paragraph from *Of Human Bondage*, by Somerset Maugham:

> Philip was sitting on the floor in the drawing-room. He was an only child and used to amusing himself. The room was filled with massive furniture, and on each of the sofas were three big cushions. These he had taken, and with the help of the chairs he had made a cave in which he could hide himself from the Red Indians. He put his ear to the floor and listened to the herd of buffaloes that raced across the prairie.

The writing is very clear. Maugham unfolds his story step by step, in simple sentences. There is no trace of any muddle. But now look at this piece of writing:

> One afternoon, when he was feeling rather bored, Mark turned down a side-street that led towards the harbour, because he decided that he would like to have a look at the sea and began making his way past the fishermen's cottages towards the sea.

There is a muddle. What did Mark do first?

> One afternoon, when he was feeling rather bored, Mark decided that he would like to have a look at the sea. He turned down a side-street that led towards the harbour and began making his way past the fishermen's cottages.

1 Here is a sentence that is not as clear as it should be because the writer has crowded too much into it:

He walked on, past a Methodist chapel and a row of small shops, until he came to the shore which was quite different from what he had expected because he had hoped to find a stretch of soft sand on which he could play, but there was only a narrow strip of mud, shut in by warehouses.

Try to rewrite it as clearly as Maugham would have written it. He would, I think, have made three sentences of it, with the middle one short. In order to re-shape it you will need to change the *which* to *it*, and leave out one of the link-words. Do not make any other changes.

2 Here is another sentence into which the writer has crowded too much. He has also arranged the order badly:

Mark stepped down onto the beach, and with his feet sinking into the wet mud he began walking out towards the water's edge but his feet did not sink far enough into the mud for it to come over the tops of his shoes.

Will you rewrite it in such a way as to get rid of the muddle. It will be best to make two sentences of it, and to deal with the matter of the feet sinking into the mud in the second one.

3 Now shape the following subject-matter into a paragraph that consists of five sentences. You will have to judge which items to merge together and which to keep separate. One item is in the wrong place (Mark *arrived* before he was *shocked*). Make only minor changes to the wording, such as putting *it* instead of *school*, and introducing link-words like *which* and *and*:

Mark was shocked when he saw what a grim place the school was. He arrived at the school just after two. He arrived a little later than he had intended. The school was surrounded by high brick walls. These walls made it look more like a prison than a school. Mark stepped up to the gate. He pressed the bell. It clanged faintly.

3

2 Sentences that get too long

Students who find writing difficult tend to make their sentences long. Why do they?

If a person is to succeed in writing a good sentence he must give some thought to what he is going to say in it, before he begins. Of course all writers, to some extent, work out their sentences as they go along. But they don't leave it *entirely* to chance. The students I have in mind do. Without thinking any further ahead than the opening idea, they start off. Then, as more ideas come to mind they put them down; and so, as they go on writing, hoping for the best, the sentence wanders on, and it turns into a long one, and as often as not, because the whole process is such a chancy business, it ends up in a muddle.

As soon as we were ready, but it took rather longer than we thought it would because it was so cold, we went out into the yard, but it was already almost completely dark which was because some heavy storm clouds had blown up from the south obscuring the sun which greatly dismayed us because we had hoped to start the drive in time to get through the Simplon Pass before it was completely dark.

If you are inclined to write sentences that are too long, it may help you if you remember these two points:

First, before you begin a sentence always pause to consider what you are going to say in it; and when you have said it put a full stop. Doing that will mean that your sentences get shorter, since it is easier to think a short way ahead than a long way.

Second, never be afraid to write a very short sentence. If what you have in mind to say comes to no more than three or four words, let that be it. *A clock struck five.* Why spoil a sentence as perfect as that one by carrying it further? *Winter came.* Why spoil that one? Or these—*A whistle blew . . . The room was empty . . . He listened . . .?*

1   Will you now complete the following passage. Write out the sentences in italics exactly as they are, and every time you come to a gap fill it in with a sentence of your own, following the suggestion that has been given. Write only one sentence for each gap. Sometimes there may be two gaps running; the end of each one is marked by a full stop.

The reader has already been told that Barry and Sarah have arranged to meet at a London railway terminal at six o'clock in the evening:

Barry arrived first, at just after five to. He glanced round. Describe the scene, mentioning only what a quick glance would reveal. Now add a touch of sharp detail to your description. *After he had been waiting for about two minutes Barry caught sight of Sarah.* Say where she was, putting her some distance away, and have her hurrying towards where Barry was waiting. Say that Barry recognized her at once because what she was wearing (say what it was) was conspicuous. *As soon as he saw her he realized that something was wrong.* Explain what it was in Sarah's manner or appearance that put this thought into his mind. *He went forward to meet her, and as they drew nearer to each other his anxiety increased.* Add a further detail about Sarah's manner or appearance, to explain this. *She stepped quickly up to him.* Now make her say something to him (just one remark), quoting what she said and starting a new paragraph for it.

2   Now write a paragraph of your own, of about the same length as the one you have just written. You could describe the scene outside a church after a wedding. . . . Or an occasion on which you saw an animal in your garden. . . . Or some street incident.

Think carefully about what you are going to say in each sentence before you begin it; and remember that if some of your sentences turn out to be very short, that is something to be pleased about.

5

3 Short sentences

Short sentences impart an air of alertness and vigour to a piece of writing. Their abruptness sharpens the impact of what is being said. So does their directness. For a short sentence is bound to be a plain blunt statement—it has no time to be anything else—and so it drives its meaning straight into the reader's mind.

Here is a fragment from a story, about a man called Raven who is on his way to assassinate a government minister. It comes from *A Gun for Sale*, by Graham Greene:

> He looked like any other young man going home after work. His dark overcoat had a clerical air. He moved steadily up the street like hundreds of his kind. You might have thought, perhaps, that he was on his way to meet his girl. But Raven had never had a girl. His hare-lip prevented that. He had learnt, when he was very young, how repulsive it was. He turned into one of the tall grey houses and climbed the stairs.

That kind of writing has a punch in it. The directness of each brief statement puts the reader on the alert. That strength would be missing, wouldn't it, if Graham Greene had written:

> Wearing a dark overcoat that had a clerical air he looked like any other young man going home after work as he moved steadily up the street like hundreds of his kind. You might have thought, perhaps, that he was on his way to meet his girl but Raven had never had a girl because his hare-lip prevented that. . . .

1   Divide the following passages into a greater number of sentences than have been used. The number into which each passage can best be divided is given in brackets. Don't alter the main trend of the wording. Make only such changes as are needed to create the divisions:

Raven stood quite still, listening intently, but the tapping continued and so he put his eye to the keyhole and peered into the dimly lit room. (3)

He went upstairs to his room, which hadn't been seen to, the bed being unmade and the ashtrays full of twisted cigarette stubs. (3)

A church clock struck five, and Raven sat up sleepily and looked out of the window. The streets were shrouded in fog which was damp and yellow and must have blown across from the river during the night. (4)

Raven walked slowly along Whitehall until he came to Trafalgar Square, where a Christmas tree stood beside Nelson's Column, hung with coloured lights and tinsel. The sight of it maddened him because even as a child he had hated the sentimentality associated with Christmas. (4)

He opened the door and peered into the room, which was quite deserted, with the knife still lying on the table, exactly where he had left it. He tip-toed across the floor to where it lay and looked closely at the blade, which had one tiny stain near the tip. (5)

He turned down a side-street and stepped into the doorway of a jeweller's shop, which, however, was not deep enough to hide him completely. He pressed his back against the glass door and listened and for a few moments everything was quiet, so that he could even hear a clock ticking inside the shop, but then, from far off, a whistle blew. (6)

2   In a paragraph about ten lines long describe a man entering a deserted building in which he suspects that somebody is hiding. Include some short sentences, to increase the tension.

4 Sentences of varying length

Long sentences demand more concentration on the part of the reader than short ones do. He has to hold more in his mind at one stretch. So they are tiring. It is not a good idea, therefore, to have too many of them in succession. No writing is more wearisome to read than a passage that consists entirely of long sentences.

Conversely, if a writer varies the length of his sentences, so that shorter ones are intermingled with longer ones, his English will be pleasant to read. It will have an air of lightness and life.

Many writers achieve pleasing effects by putting sentences of contrasting length next to each other. Here is some more of the story we looked at last time, with Raven still on his way to murder the government minister:

> He turned into one of the tall grey houses and climbed the stairs. Outside the top flat he put down his attaché case, took a pair of clippers out of his pocket, and cut through the telephone wire where it ran out from above the door to the lift shaft. Then he rang the bell.

Because of the contrast in length, that little sentence at the end has an added sharpness. The reader is pulled up by it, after his long journey through the previous sentence, and made to pause.

> He came out into Deer Street. It was deserted. The rows of shops were boarded up. He took a quick look in both directions, and then pulling his coat collar up as high as it would go he strode forward into the wind.

There, it is the long sentence that benefits from the contrast. After the restraint of the short, clipped statements that lead up to it, it has an air of expansiveness and freedom.

1   Divide these passages into sentences of contrasting length. Make only minor adjustments to the wording:

As she turned round she caught sight of his hare-lip and she winced slightly and looked the other way, in a clumsy attempt to disguise her feelings, which infuriated him. (Three sentences—the last one very short)

As soon as he came out into Frith Street, where the light was brighter, he took out his handkerchief and covered his mouth, this being his only chance. (Long, short)

He went upstairs and rang the bell of one of the doors on the first floor and it was opened by a nurse whose uniform needed washing and she brought with her a smell of chemicals. (Three sentences—the middle one short)

November came, and on most evenings now, as he walked back to his digs from the station, a foggy dampness lay over the streets, which brought back the ache in his hip. (Short, long, short)

They dined in Soho, Raven choosing the restaurant, one of those little crowded places where they kept the lights dimmed so as to hide the seediness in a romantic gloom. (Short, short, long)

2   Will you now write a paragraph in which you describe a sequence of events. Choose any subject you like. (Two people might be keeping an appointment to meet— furtively, perhaps, in a city street. . . . Or perhaps a detective is trailing a suspect. . . . Or a commuter might be returning to his lodgings. . . . Or someone might be carefully hiding something away . . .). Introduce into your paragraph at least one sharp contrast between a long sentence and a short one.

5   Sentences that end strongly

When we write a sentence the natural thing to do is to put
the important point first, because it is uppermost in our
mind; and then we add whatever else we want to say:

> The little village of Bream lay half a mile further on,
> just out of sight behind a screen of hazel and ash.

That is the natural order. But we are not obliged to
follow it. We can keep the main point till the end:

> Half a mile further on, just out of sight behind a screen
> of hazel and ash, lay the little village of Bream.

A writer's purpose, when he shapes a sentence in that
way, is to build up a sense of expectation, so that when
he finally does come out with his main point it has an
added force.

This is a useful piece of technique to keep in mind if you
want to increase the emphasis of a statement:

> Lies of this sort poison the mind, from whatever
> quarter they come, and however plausibly they may be
> presented.

> Lies of this sort, from whatever quarter they come, and
> however plausibly they may be presented, poison the
> mind.

It may be useful, too, if you want to heighten the drama
of some event you are describing:

> Suddenly he stood still and listened. A child was calling
> from far away, with a cry so faint that he could only
> just catch the sound of it.

> Suddenly he stood still and listened. From far away,
> with a cry so faint that he could only just catch the
> sound of it, a child was calling.

1   Here are some pieces of writing by various authors. In each passage I have altered *one* of the sentences by rearranging the order of the words. As the author wrote the sentence, it ended strongly, with the main point kept back till the end: I have put the main point either at the beginning or near the beginning. Will you look through each passage, decide which sentence has been altered, and then rewrite that sentence as the author wrote it. Change only the order – not the words themselves. A few minor adjustments to the punctuation may be needed:

There was a silence on the river as the *Swallow* drifted on.

"I see it. I see it," cried Roger.

On the front of the boathouse was a huge skull-and-cross-bones, high up over the entrance, cut out of wood and painted staring white. (From *Swallows and Amazons*, by Arthur Ransome)

One afternoon the Rector appeared in the doorway, when a pitched battle was raging among the big boys in the class and the mistress was calling imploringly for order.

"Silence!" he roared.

The silence was immediate and profound, for they knew he was not to be trifled with. (From *Lark Rise to Candleford*, by Flora Thompson)

He had promised me a silver fourpenny on the first of every month if I would keep my eye open for a sea-faring man with one leg, and let him know the moment he appeared. But often enough he would only blow through his nose at me and stare me down, when the first of the month came round and I applied to him for my wage. (From *Treasure Island*, by R. L. Stevenson)

Many people regarded the Chancellor as a mouse when he took office last January. But already he has become a major political figure, just six months later, to the astonishment of everyone. (From a newspaper article)

11

6 Incomplete sentences: introduced accidentally

When we speak we do not always bother to phrase our
language in the form of complete sentences. We have no
need to, because as well as words we have gestures and
expressions and tone of voice to help us explain our
meaning. We can break off in the middle of a sentence
and complete the sense by a look, or by a turn of the
head or a shrug of the shoulders. In writing it is different.
There, we have only the words on the page. So it is
accepted that usually, when we are writing, we express
ourselves in language that is continuous and complete.

Now here is a passage in which the writer did *not* do
that:

> The Amazon is tremendously wide at this point. More
> like a huge lake than a river, could even be the ocean:
> No sign of the opposite bank. Except that the steady
> flow of the water towards the east gives it the look of a
> river.

Why did all those sentences, except the first one, turn out
to be incomplete? It was because the writer, without
realizing it was happening, allowed his writing to be
shaped by the habits of casual everyday chat. Incomplete
sentences like those, appearing accidentally and serving
no purpose, not only make the writing seem slovenly:
they also, quite often, make it harder to understand.

> The Amazon is tremendously wide at this point. It
> looks more like a huge lake than a river, or even like
> the ocean, for there is no sign of the opposite bank.
> Only the steady flow of the water towards the east gives
> it the look of a river.

In each of the following pieces of writing some of the sentences are incomplete because the writer, instead of shaping his language with care, allowed the habits of casual everyday speech to determine what he wrote. Will you rewrite each passage, in full, in the form of complete sentences and in fluent English.

The incomplete sentences are printed in italics. You should make each one complete either by arranging for there to be a main verb in it (that is, a verb round which a sentence can be built), or else by joining it to what comes before it or to what follows it:

Dorset has a wide variety of scenery. *Probably more than any other county in England. In some parts green valleys stretching for many miles, threaded with small streams.* In other places bare uplands rise to heights of nearly nine hundred feet. *Also a long and beautiful coastline, which in itself is richly varied.*

He was a very old man. He started talking to me about the past. *About his schooldays. How he used to leave home at eight in the morning to make the journey to school. A penny ride on the tram.* It was strange to listen to him. *Seeing his eyes light up as his imagination took him back to those distant days.*

I spend a lot of time enticing animals into our small suburban garden. *Among the regular visitors, two hedgehogs and one fox. The attraction being the bowl of milk I put out every evening.* From time to time there have been other visitors too. I have seen a shrew and a fieldmouse. *Also a badger. Just once, about a year ago.* He approached the bowl, sniffed at it, and then turned and walked away through the hedge. *Being no lover of milk, apparently.*

7   Incomplete sentences in newspapers

Journalists on popular newspapers often write incomplete sentences. Their purpose, usually, is to suggest that they are just chatting to us in a natural way:

> The Red revolution has come at last. Nothing to be frightened about though. Because it comes in the shape of Mrs Annie Powell, who has been described as 'a lovely lady'. Red Annie is to be Britain's first Communist mayor. In Rhondda. Nice for Annie. Nice for the country. Nice to know that not all Communists are ugly customers.

The person who wrote that paragraph wants us to feel that we are listening to a matey sort of bloke who has a line of smart talk. He knew what he was doing. The writing seems to be an exact reproduction of his breezy chat. But it is not. On the contrary it has been carefully shaped, and made very clear and very easy to read. Impromptu talk is not as tidy as that.

An 'incomplete' style of that kind, deliberately contrived, is quite different from the style of that piece of writing we looked at on page 12, about the Amazon. There, the incompleteness came accidentally, through mere slackness, and the English is merely slovenly.

1   Here are some pieces of writing that have been picked out of newspapers because they have incomplete sentences in them. Will you re-shape them in the form of continuous English, making all the sentences complete.

The purpose of doing this is not to improve the passages, but to reveal the special style in which they are written. In a sense it would not be possible to improve them (except within the terms of this style) since the journalists who wrote them achieved the effect they were after—a flow of slick, chatty English:

After thirty years of decline cinema audiences are booming again. 'House full' signs outside the doors on Saturday evenings. Queues stretching half way down the High Streets. Splendid. People are getting bored with too much telly. Especially young people. We wish them luck. Good to get away from the house occasionally and have a night out.

So this obstinate ex-Minister has decided to retire to the back benches. The very move that no one expected him to make. Typical.

The Communist Party of Russia deplores the 'decadent' music of the west. Not so the Russian people. The welcome they gave to this multi-millionaire singer was tremendous. Even bigger than the welcome he received on his American tour last year.

The Foreign Secretary advised caution. Very statesman-like. A fine, dignified speech. But caution is sometimes a form of weakness. Or cowardice.

It was the world's tallest wedding cake. Sixteen storeys high. Three hundredweight of icing and marzipan. Standing on the front lawn because it was too big to go into the house. The newly wedded pair mounted a ladder together and cut a tiny piece out of the top tier. Their first slice of luck.

2   Write a short paragraph of sales-talk, in the 'incomplete' style, for an advertisement.

8 Incomplete sentences: introduced as a contrast

> One of the most mysterious episodes in the life of this strange, ascetic woman was her brief marriage. It was a disaster that was to leave its mark on her for the rest of her days. One might have expected that the author of this 'definitive' biography would have enquired into the mystery of this marriage, and might perhaps have had something interesting to say about it. Nothing doing. He doesn't even mention it.

There, the incomplete sentence comes in as a piece of colloquial bluntness, suddenly appearing in a context of fluent, cultured English. The contrast is very effective. It brings a touch of down-to-earth vigour into the writing.

Here is another example:

> His hair is white now, and he leans forward when you speak to him for he has gone partially deaf. But he still gets up every morning at seven and does an hour's writing before breakfast, in a style that has as much vigour in it as ever. Perhaps more.

There, incompleteness and brevity combine to isolate those last two little words and load them with emphasis.

Using incomplete sentences in this way, occasionally, as a means of forceful contrast, is quite a different matter from using them continually as a chatty mannerism, in the way that writers do in popular newspapers or in advertisements.

1 Here is a passage in which several of the sentences are incomplete. They are incomplete not because the writer deliberately wrote them in that way, to achieve some purpose, but because, without realizing that he was doing it, he allowed the habits of casual talk to shape them like that. Will you rewrite the passage in the form of complete sentences. You can change the wording here and there if you think it necessary, but do not alter the meaning:

Swimming underwater with the aid of a breathing tube is a sport that opens up new and strange experiences. One moment sitting on a noisy, crowded beach, a few seconds later gliding through a silent world of marine life. Fish dart away from you as you propel yourself forward by means of the fins on your feet. Soft, sponge-like shapes floating past, within a few inches of your face. It is a world of wonderful colours. The purples and greens of the seaweed, for example, the pink tentacles of the anemones waving in the water. You need very little equipment. Just a snorkel, a face mask, and fins.

2 Here is another piece of writing in which the style is marred by the same fault. Will you improve it in the same way as you improved the previous passage:

One of the most difficult climbs in the world is the ascent of the south-west face of Everest. The climb made by Chris Bonington and his team in 1975. Among the hazards they had to face were bitterly cold temperatures and a violent wind. Especially the wind, which blows fiercely against this side of the mountain nearly all the time, often making it impossible for a climber to move at all. Also the steepness of the ascent, for this is the most precipitous mountain face in the world.

9 Incomplete sentences in descriptive passages

Writers sometimes go in for the literary device of leaving out the verbs in a descriptive passage. They just name the features that make up the scene, so that the description becomes like a list:

> Twilight upon meadow and water. The eve-star shining above the hill, and Old Nog the heron crying *kra-a-ark*! A whiteness drifting above the sere reeds of the riverside. (From *Tarka the Otter*, by Henry Williamson)

> No wind, and the grey sea calm and full. Campion in bloom in the hedges, and the air mild. (From *The Birds*, by Daphne du Maurier)

> From my window, the deep solemn massive street. Cellar-shops where the lamps burn all day. Dirty plaster frontages embossed with scrollwork and heraldic devices. (From *Goodbye to Berlin*, by Christopher Isherwood)

> A student's room in the Hotel de l'Avenir. Piles of books everywhere—on tables, chairs, and in heaps on the floor. On the wall a faded photograph of Capri. (From *The Story of San Michele*, by Axel Munthe)

The purpose of a writer, perhaps, when he writes in that way, is to make his description seem like a picture which he is in the very act of painting, stroke by stroke.

This is a device that is used only rarely. One has to search a long way in order to find examples of it. Some people, perhaps, might regard it as being rather self-conscious or precious.

1   Will you rewrite the following passages in such a way as to make all the sentences complete. The purpose is not to improve the descriptions, but to reveal, by means of the contrast, the 'sketchy' style in which they are written. As you finish each passage compare your 'complete' version with the original one, and decide which of the two you like better:

At last the curtain parted, and there he was, seated ready. A big, round rock of a man. His face lit by a smile that showed a row of gleaming teeth. His dark skin catching the light and shining like polished wood. On his knee the nine-string guitar from which in a moment those whining treble notes would be so deftly plucked.

I can still remember our house in Streatham. A Victorian house with high railings in front of it. The entrance hall very large, and a wide staircase rising up from the far corner of it. On the left a door leading into my father's room, and at the far end another door that opened out into the garden.

Standing here at the window I can look along the whole length of the street. It is a picturesque sight. On the left, quite near, the timbered front of the Lion Hotel. It sags and wavers like cardboard. Beyond it, standing strongly upright, the iron arches of the covered market. Beyond that, on either side, small shops and cafés, and furthest away of all, at the far end of the street, the grey block of the ancient church. Behind it, in the distance, rising gently up, the green slopes of the downs.

2   Now write two versions of a description of your own. Describe a fairly static scene; don't include any happenings. Write the first version in the 'sketchy' style, making most of the sentences incomplete, and the second one in the form of complete sentences.

10 Incomplete sentences: when should you write them?

The advice must be 'never', or 'hardly ever'. Let us look again at the four kinds we have described.

Introduced accidentally. Incomplete sentences that turn up in a person's writing by accident are almost certain to have a bad effect on it. They nearly always make it seem slapdash and poorly conceived.

In popular newspapers. The impression that is given is that we are listening to the slick chat of a smart talker. It is not likely that you will often want to achieve that effect.

Introduced as a contrast. Introducing an incomplete sentence for this purpose—as a sudden intrusion of colloquial vigour—makes for very strong writing. But it takes a great deal of skill to achieve a contrast of this kind. It is bound to, because the contrast is between a flow of cultured English and a piece of carefully chosen— and carefully timed—colloquial directness. So you need to be a master of the whole range of the language. But there is no reason why you should not try for this effect if you want to—as long as you understand clearly what you are aiming for.

In descriptive passages. Perhaps you like those descriptions that are like lists? If you do, there is absolutely no reason why you should not introduce them into your writing, occasionally.

1   In the following piece of writing there are several incomplete sentences. None of them serve any purpose, and they spoil the English. Some of them cause a confusion of meaning. Will you rewrite the passage in the form of complete sentences. You can change the wording if you think it necessary, and also the order in which the ideas are expressed, but do not alter what the writer has said:

According to many scientists the universe is expanding, all the time, at an enormous speed. Because of a huge explosion that occurred billions of years ago. Like a balloon being blown bigger and bigger but never bursting. By means of modern telescopes we can calculate the age of the universe. Probably about twelve billion years old. Although possibly, according to some scientists, even older than that. During the course of its existence innumerable galaxies of stars have been formed, through the condensation of vast clouds of gas. One of which is the Milky Way.

2   Here is another passage which is spoilt by the same fault. Will you improve it in the same way as you improved the previous passage:

In recent years an increasing interest has been taken in what might be called the 'natural' sports. Meaning by this, sports in which a person tests his skill against the forces of nature. Like hang-gliding, for example, or surfing. Another one is white-water canoeing. Of these the most dangerous is hang-gliding. The only way to learn is to go to a properly registered school and obtain a pilot's certificate. You begin with tethered flights. Extending up to fifty feet in the air, lasting about fifteen minutes, and controlled from the ground by an instructor who is linked to you by radio. Soon you may be allowed to fly solo. Could even be after only three or four tethered flights. *If* you have mastered the control bar.

11   Misleading sentences

A writer, guiding his readers along the path of a sentence, should never lead them down a false trail. On the contrary, he should make sure that every step of the way is absolutely clear.

As soon as they came out into the open smoke, mixed with gas and other fumes, began to pour out of the building.

The reader is tricked into taking a wrong turning.

An otter curled in the dry upper hollow of the fallen oak heard them, and uncurling, shook herself on four short legs. (From *Tarka the Otter*, by Henry Williamson)

Curled starts us off along a wrong path.

All round him the long scar smashed into the jungle was a bath of heat. (From *Lord of the Flies*, by William Golding)

So does *smashed*.

Then she bent down and washed her hands and her wedding-ring—which was loose anyhow—began to slip off. (From *August is a Wicked Month*, by Edna O'Brien)

The second *and* is misleading.

In the next example the hitch is so minute that some people might consider it too trifling to be worth mentioning. Well, one could quote Michelangelo's words: 'Perfection is achieved by attending to trifles; but perfection itself is no trifle.'

Then, like all dreamers, I was possessed of a sudden with supernatural powers. (From *Rebecca*, by Daphne du Maurier)

Will you now rewrite those five misleading sentences in such a way that the reader is not misled. Here are a few suggestions to help you:

As soon as they came out . . .: a change in the punctuation will clear up the muddle.

An otter curled . . .: again, a change in the punctuation will settle the matter; or else the punctuation could be left as it is and two words could be added after 'otter'.

All round him . . . add three words after 'scar'.

Then she bent down and washed . . .: a change in the punctuation is all that is needed.

Then, like all dreamers . . .: *of,* when it comes after *possessed,* is usually followed by what is possessed (*He was possessed of a large fortune*); so for an infinitesimal instant the reader takes *sudden* for a noun (the thing that is possessed).

Words

12   Adjectives that contribute nothing

'Be a miser with adjectives,' wrote Eden Phillpots. It is good advice, for they are words that are very easy to come by. Often they slip into a person's writing when they are not needed and weaken the nouns they describe instead of strengthening them. That is what Voltaire meant when he said they were the enemies of nouns.

> I admired his tremendous courage. . . . We were entranced by the wonderful beauty of the scene. . . . I still remember the excitement I felt when I first read this very interesting story.

The adjectives in those sentences fall on the ear with a dead sound because all they do is add a superfluous comment. If you read the sentences through again and leave the adjectives out, you will see the improvement.

Whenever you use an adjective you should make sure that either you need it in order to convey your meaning, or else that it adds a touch of genuine enrichment. What you should guard against, continually, is allowing your writing to become cluttered with adjectives which merely add feeble comments.

Here is a paragraph from *The Slave*, by Isaac Bashevis Singer. The adjectives are printed in italics:

> The sun had moved westward; the day was nearing its end. The sky was still *clear*, but a *milk-white* fog was forming in the woods. Jacob could see for miles around. The mountains remained as *deserted* as in the days of the Creation. One above the other, the forests rose, first the *leaf-bearing* trees, and then the pines and firs.

All those adjectives except one have a simple and definite meaning. The author introduced them not to enrich his description but because he needed them in order to be able to say what he wanted to say. Which one did he introduce to enrich the picture?

26

1 In this next extract from *The Slave* the author used
two adjectives. I have spoilt it by adding five more—all of
them superfluous. Will you rewrite it as he wrote it,
without my adjectives. Then read through what you have
written and see how much better it is without them:

It stormed in the middle of the night. A *sudden* flash of
lightning lit up the interior of the barn, and the cows,
dung heaps, and earthen pots became *visible* for a *brief*
instant. Thunder rumbled, and a *strong* gust of wind
blew open the barn door. The *heavy* downpour beat on
the roof like hail. The *driving* rain lashed Jacob as he
closed and latched the door. He built a *small* fire, and
sat by it praying.

This extract and the next two are quoted correctly on
page 42.

2 In each of the following extracts three superfluous
adjectives have been added to what Isaac Bashevis Singer
wrote. Will you rewrite each passage without them.
There are no italics to help you this time:

After a while the wagon entered a beautiful pine-wood,
which seemed less a forest than some heavenly mansion.
The trees were as tall and straight as pillars, and the
sky leaned on their green tops. The light which filtered
through shone with all the wonderful colours of the
rainbow. Jacob closed his eyes as though begrudging
himself the sight of such great splendour.

Wandering through the narrow street, Jacob saw how
great the poverty was. Many lived in what were only
dark burrows; tradesmen worked in shops that looked
like wretched kennels. A horrible stench rose from the
filthy gutters.

3 Now write a description, about ten lines long, of some
outdoor scene (by the sea? . . . a fair? . . . a street scene?
. . . a sports meeting? . . .) Try to achieve the effect you
want without using many adjectives, and make sure that
any you do use contribute something worthwhile.

13   Vague adjectives

Some are so vague that they can be applied to almost anything:

> It was a dreadful journey . . . a dreadful play . . . dreadful weather. . . .

We could be more precise:

> It was a tiring journey . . . a tedious journey . . . a dangerous journey . . . a scandalous play . . . squally weather.

General adjectives like *dreadful* are not always bad. Sometimes they help one's thoughts to flow. All writers use them now and then. But it is a good idea to pause, if you find that you are about to use one, and ask yourself if perhaps you might do better by being more specific.

There is another reason for being wary of them. Because they are so easy to come by they are heavily overworked, and so any life they might once have had has long since gone out of them. *Awful, horrible, terrible, marvellous, lovely, tremendous, nice*—the feeblest writer in the world has adjectives like those at his finger-tips.

1   Will you now write down all the adjectives which come in this passage. It is taken from *Cider with Rosie*, by Laurie Lee. There are nine. Then underline the two which you consider to be the most generalized:

My father left us when I was an infant, and apart from fugitive visits he did not live with us again. He was a brisk, elusive man, the son and the grandson of sailors. He became, while still in his teens, a grocer's assistant, a church organist, a photographer, and a dandy. The portraits he took of himself at that time show a handsome lad, tall and slender, much addicted to gloves, stiff collars, and courtly poses. By the age of twenty he had married the beautiful daughter of a merchant.

2   In the next passage three of the adjectives Laurie Lee used have been left out. Will you suggest one to fill each space. All three of them are to do with the heat. There is no question of your being asked to try and hit on the exact words he used—no one could do that; but when you have made your suggestions compare your choice with his. The passage, which comes from *I Can't Stay Long*, is quoted in full on page 42.

In Florence the spring was over and the heat had come. The carved palaces quivered like radiators in the sun. _____ blasts of air, as from kitchen stoves, moved through the streets laden with odours of meat and frying oil. In the cheaper cafés _____ British tourists sat sweating and counting their crumpled money. But from the tower of the Palazzo Vecchio one could look out across the _____ roofs of the city and see the rising hills around.

3   Now, in about five or six lines of writing, describe an afternoon of stifling heat (in a classroom? . . . in a street? . . . in a train? . . .). Choose your adjectives extra carefully, and do not use too many.

14 Hackneyed adjectives

Some adjectives go so well with certain nouns that they are always being used to describe them:

Grim determination . . . a stormy meeting . . . a yawning gap . . . a striking example . . . a valiant attempt . . . a gripping story. . . .

There is nothing vague about those adjectives. You would not say to anyone who used them, 'Be more precise'. But because they are used so often they are ineffective. We feel, when we come across one, that the writer may have chosen it from force of habit rather than because he thought it suitable. He may have been using it sincerely, but we have no way of knowing, and so we do not trust him.

It is better not to allow adjective-and-noun couples of that kind to get into your writing, for they are nothing more than somebody else's worn out expressions.

1 Here are two descriptive passages:

She looked up to where the *sombre* splendour of Vesuvius, rising from the fields of lava and ashes, was smoking against the *clear* blue of the sky. Amid the *peaceful* loveliness it struck a *discordant* note of danger. She left the terrace to walk into the garden amidst the *fragrant* petals of the *blossoming* shrubs. As she moved she disturbed a profusion of *colourful* butterflies who with the bees were hovering over the *open* blooms.

Out in the King's Ride the pheasants were being driven across the noses of the guns. Up they spurted from the underwood like *heavy* rockets, and as they rose the guns cracked in order, eagerly, sharply, as if a line of dogs had suddenly barked. Tufts of *white* smoke held together for a moment; then gently dissolved themselves, faded, and dispersed.

In the road a cart stood, laid already with *soft warm* bodies, with *limp* claws, and still *lustrous* eyes. The birds seemed alive still, but swooning under their *rich damp* feathers.

Will you write out both the passages, leaving out every adjective that can possibly be left out. If an adjective is necessary to the sense, then obviously it must stay; but an adjective must also stay if it is one that contributes something worthwhile to the picture, and if leaving it out would spoil the effect.

If any of the sentences are going to remain unaltered, write only the first and last words and put dots between. The names of the authors of the passages are given on page 42, but do not look until you have done the question.

2 Write a paragraph, of about the same length as those we have just quoted, in which you describe the scene at one of these places: a riverside restaurant, a harbour, an airport, a swimming pool. Be sparing with your adjectives and choose them carefully.

15   Adverbs

Adverbs sometimes find their way into a person's writing when they do no more than duplicate the meaning of some other word in the sentence:

> He hurried quickly down the steps. . . . The glass crashed noisily onto the pavement. . . . The trees were heavily laden with fruit.

The adverbs are not needed. All they do is clutter up the English.

Some adverbs are vague and generalized. That same gang, that we met as adjectives, turn up again as adverbs:

> Awfully thin . . . dreadfully unhappy . . . terrifically brave . . . tremendously tall . . . terribly hot. . . .

Adverbs of that kind are sometimes useful. But often they are not needed, and they weaken the writing; and the best thing to do is to cross them out. At other times, if a qualifying word *is* needed, a *very* or an *extremely* will probably be better, or a more precise adverb:

> Very thin . . . pitifully thin . . . horrifyingly thin . . . deeply unhappy . . . extremely brave . . . majestically tall . . . oppressively hot.

There are also some hackneyed expressions in which the hackneyed word is the adverb. It is best to avoid them:

> Desperately anxious . . . blissfully happy . . . abysmally ignorant . . . disarmingly frank . . . breathtakingly beautiful. . . .

1   In four of the following sentences the adverb is superfluous. Will you decide which those four are, and rewrite them without the adverb:

The field sloped steeply down to a sandy bay. . . . A thin rain was pattering softly on the leaves. . . . She worked quickly, concentrating her whole attention on the task. . . . A gigantic wave crashed violently against the pier. . . . He eyed her curiously, wondering if she would remember him. . . . The wet grass glinted brightly in the sunshine. . . . For the rest of the afternoon it rained steadily. . . . In the distance a spike of rock jutted sharply into the skyline.

2   Will you now suggest adjectives and adverbs to fill the spaces in the next passage. It comes from *Odour of Chrysanthemums*, by D. H. Lawrence. The purpose is not to try and guess the words he used, but to suggest words of your own; nevertheless, when you have finished, you may like to compare your choice with his by turning to page 42.

The small locomotive engine came clanking down from Selston with seven full wagons. It appeared round the corner with _____ threats of speed, but the colt that it startled from among the gorse outdistanced it at a canter. A woman, walking up the railway line to Underwood, drew back into the hedge, held her basket aside, and watched the footplate of the engine advancing. The trucks thumped _____ly past, one by one, with a slow _____ movement, as she stood insignificantly trapped between the jolting black wagons and the hedge. Then they curved away towards the coppice where the _____ oak leaves dropped _____ly, while the birds, pulling at the scarlet hips beside the track, made off into the dusk. In the open, smoke from the engine sank and cleaved to the _____ grass. The fields were _____ and forsaken. Beyond them the pit-bank loomed up, flames like _____ sores licking its ashy sides, in the afternoon's _____ light.

16   *Very* and some other words

Very has little power: it is used too often. People sometimes try to strengthen it by underlining it ('It was *very*
hot'), but doing that makes it seem weaker than ever.
So if we want to sharpen the emphasis we have to look
for a more precise word ('oppressively hot'? . . . 'unbear-
ably hot'? . . . 'blindingly hot'?), or else find some other
way of expressing ourselves (a simile perhaps).

There are several other general words, in the same
category as *very*, which are just as easy to come by—
words like *rather, quite, completely, extremely*. They are
useful sometimes, and they are harmless. Some others are
not so harmless. *Somewhat* is pompous ('The prospect was
somewhat alarming'). *Definitely* is nearly always used,
quite wrongly, as though it meant that there was no doubt
about something ('He was definitely born under a lucky
star'). And *really* has an odd way, sometimes, of suggest-
ing that the writer is trying his utmost to convey his
meaning but that his vocabulary is too limited for him to
be able to manage it ('It really was a wonderful sight').

General words of the kind we have been looking at are
often useful, but they are not the stuff of which strong
writing is made. Strong writing is always particularized
and precise.

1   The following extract—from *Over to You*, by Roald Dahl—has been slightly altered. It contains seven general words of the kind we have been considering. He used only one. This one, though not necessary, is acceptable. All the others have an unwanted look. Which one did he use? You can check your answer by turning to page 42.

The Battle of Athens was perhaps the very last of the great dog-fighting air battles that will ever be fought. Nowadays one does not dog-fight at all over the sky except on very rare occasions. But the Battle of Athens was a rather long and extremely beautiful dog-fight, in which fifteen Hurricanes fought two hundred German bombers and fighters. The bombers started coming over fairly early in the afternoon. It was a really lovely spring day. The sky was really blue, save for a very few wispy clouds.

2   Here is another extract from the same book:

The Spitfire pilot was looking around him into the sky. As he screwed up his eyes and searched he saw a small black speck moving slowly across the bright surface of the sun, and to him the speck was not a speck but a life-size German pilot sitting in a Focke Wulf which had cannon in its wings. There was not much time. The Focke Wulf came out of the sun with its nose down and it came fast.

The outcome of the fight was as follows: the Focke Wulf flew straight at the Spitfire, firing at it; their wingtips touched, accidentally; a wing of the Spitfire was torn off, and the pilot baled out and parachuted. Will you describe these events, from the point of view of the Spitfire pilot, in a paragraph of between 50 and 100 words. As you write your account take care not to use *very* or any other of those general words we have been considering, unless they are needed. Make sure, too, that any adjectives or adverbs you introduce are well chosen.

17 Too many words

Here is a piece of writing:

There could be no doubt that Walter was a terribly self-conscious type of person. When there was a party going on and everyone in the room started singing songs or something like that, he never joined in with the fun because he could never bring himself to do that. It was just not in his nature. He sat there smiling round at everyone to show he was pleased, but it was quite obvious to all those present that his smile was only put on because you could see it was forced.

That is a spoilt version of something that was written by Somerset Maugham. This is what he wrote:

Walter was self-conscious. When there was a party going on and everyone started singing, he could never bring himself to join in. He sat there smiling to show he was pleased, but his smile was forced.

If you use more words than are needed to say something you weaken the force of your writing. You also try the patience of your reader. A good writer weighs up what he writes, and he takes care not to include in it anything that is empty. This is not to say that he never allows himself a lightweight sentence here and there, or a little word like a *very* or a *rather*. These are relaxations, and he includes them if they help his writing to flow. But he eliminates any wordiness that spoils it.

People never write *too* sparely. It is not possible to, because economy of style is not a fault. But it is only too easy to go the other way, and become lazily expansive, and let the pages fill up nice and quickly, because one is not bothering to do the hard thinking that is needed to sort out what is worth saying from what is not. That is the commonest fault there is.

1   The following passages are 'filled out' versions of pieces of writing by well known authors. Will you rewrite them, leaving out any words that you think are superfluous. Do not make any other changes (except adjustments to the punctuation). The number of words 'saved' by the authors is given in brackets at the end of each passage, and the original versions are given on page 72:

Macalister's boy took one of the fish and cut a whole square piece out of its side to bait his hook with. The poor creature's mutilated body (it was alive still, even after having had that done to it) was thrown back into the sea to die a lingering death. (From *To the Lighthouse*, by Virginia Woolf, who used 17 words fewer.)

In the morning they buried Mrs Collard. The serjeant got a coolie, and he dug a shallow grave to lay her in. When it was ready they lowered her into it covered with a blanket, and Mrs Horsefall read a little out of the Prayer Book. Then, when she had finished, they took away the blanket so that it should not get buried, because they could not spare that, and the earth was filled in over Mrs Collard's body. (From *A Town Like Alice*, by Nevil Shute, who used 23 words fewer.)

2   Now here is a passage which has *not* been filled out. It is given as Barbara Cartland wrote it (in *The Dream and the Glory*):

Then, as if he could not help himself or resist the invitation of Cordelia's arms, his mouth came down on hers. He was trying to be gentle; he was trying, she knew, to keep control of himself. But a flame within her seemed to leap higher and as it rose it ignited a fire in him, so that his kisses became fierce, demanding masterful and wildly passionate.

Some people might feel, perhaps, that she used too many words. Will you rewrite it, leaving out any that you think are not needed (possibly 21 or 22 of them). Do not make any other changes.

37

18 Slang

The author of this excellent book has made a lifetime's study of film history, and the knowledge he has accumulated is tempered by a fine sense of judgement. He devotes a whole chapter to an analysis of horror films. These films, according to him, do much more than just frighten the pants off us: they enable us to indulge our fantasies and exorcise our fears.

Using a slang expression in that way is fine. The writer introduced it in order to give the paragraph a bit of punch. And why does it succeed in doing that? It succeeds because it is set, not in a context of more slang, but amidst a flow of cultured English. The vigour comes from the contrast.

There is another way of using slang expressions: the way of someone who uses them not just occasionally, as a contrast, but all the time, because they are the first words that come to mind and using them saves the trouble of looking any further:

The author has put a terrific lot into this book and he comes up with some pretty good ideas. He really goes to town over horror films. According to him these films help you get rid of hang-ups as well as frightening the pants off you.

Where is the contrast in that passage? Writing of that kind, hovering always on the verge of slang, does not make for any vigour at all: on the contrary it suggests, drearily, that the writer is incapable of lifting his style above the level of chat.

It is not easy to use slang effectively. To succeed, you need to have a command of the whole range of the language, since success depends on achieving a contrast between the careless spontaneity of everyday language and the disciplined fluency of writing.

Now write a paragraph, not more than half a page long, about one of the following subjects, or about any other subject you like to choose: a well known book . . . tower blocks . . . winning a fortune . . . old films . . . the radio.

Write it in simple, clear English that has no trace of chattiness or slang in it, but try to introduce just one slang expression as a contrast. The expression could possibly be in the form of an incomplete sentence, if it suited you to have it that way – like the incomplete sentence that comes in the first extract on page 16.

19   Pompous words

Some people, so as to be sure of not relapsing into a
chatty style of writing, try to sound learned and
literary. They adopt a pompous manner; and they
end up by making themselves look ridiculous.

Here are two versions of a description of some caves.
The second one is what E. M. Forster wrote in *A Passage
to India*:

> The caves tend to be somewhat obscured by an all-
> prevailing darkness. Even in those instances in which
> their apertures face in the direction of the sun, only a
> minimal amount of light penetrates into the circular
> chamber. There is not a great deal to see, and no eye
> to see it, until a visitor appears on the scene and
> momentarily illuminates the cave by igniting a match.

> They are dark caves. Even when they open towards the
> sun, very little light penetrates into the circular chamber.
> There is little to see, and no eye to see it, until a visitor
> arrives and strikes a match.

A good piece of writing will have been written with
care, and this care will be bound to have raised it above
the level of casual chattiness. That—and that alone—will
be the secret of its dignity. There is no question of its
having to be high-sounding in order to be dignified. On the
contrary, the very best kind of writing can be utterly
simple, and can seem to have come as naturally as speech
comes. But the speech it will remind us of will not be the
casual talk of everyday life: it will sound like someone
speaking who has chosen his words wisely and carefully.

1   Now rewrite these sentences. In each one, substitute a single, simple word for the italicized word or group of words:

He made a *somewhat lengthy* speech. . . . There were *approximately* a dozen empty seats. . . . The boys were *endeavouring* to drag the log up the bank. . . . The film was *excessively* long. . . . I live quite near this famous palace and I have visited it *on numerous occasions*. . . . Few people *anticipated* that the war would last so long. . . . This land has been *purchased* by the National Trust.

2   We have looked at the next passage, which was written by Somerset Maugham, earlier in this book. In the version you are now going to read, four of his words have been replaced by longer ones. Can you tell which these longer words are? Write them down, and suggest four simpler ones which would express the same meaning. Then turn to page 2 to see what Maugham wrote:

Philip was sitting on the floor in the drawing-room. He was an only child and accustomed to amusing himself. The room was filled with massive furniture, and on each of the sofas were three big cushions. These he had taken, and with the help of the chairs he had constructed a cave in which he could conceal himself from the Red Indians. He applied his ear to the floor and listened to the herd of buffaloes that raced across the prairie.

3   Now rewrite this sentence in a style that is as plain and simple as you can make it:

Throughout the duration of the summer months Haworth tends to be crowded with numerous visitors, and these crowds render it somewhat difficult to comprehend the degree of loneliness and quietness the place must have enjoyed in the time of the Brontës.

Correct versions of quoted extracts

Page 27—Question 1
It stormed in the middle of the night. A flash of lightning lit up the interior of the barn, and the cows, dung heaps, and earthen pots became visible for an instant. Thunder rumbled, and a gust of wind blew open the barn door. The downpour beat on the roof like hail. The rain lashed Jacob as he closed and latched the door. He built a small fire, and sat by it praying.

Page 27—Question 2
After a while the wagon entered a pine-wood, which seemed less a forest than some heavenly mansion. The trees were as tall and straight as pillars, and the sky leaned on their green tops. The light which filtered through shone with all the colours of the rainbow. Jacob closed his eyes as though begrudging himself the sight of such splendour.

Wandering through the narrow streets, Jacob saw how great the poverty was. Many lived in what were only dark burrows; tradesmen worked in shops that looked like kennels. A stench rose from the gutters.

Page 29—Question 2
Hot blasts of air, as from kitchen stoves, moved through the streets. . . . In the cheaper cafés brick-faced British tourists sat sweating . . . . . . one could look out across the roasting roofs of the city and see the rising hills around.

Page 31—Question 1
Barbara Cartland: *The Dream and the Glory*. Virginia Woolf: *The Shooting Party*.

Page 33—Question 2
It appeared round the corner with loud threats of speed. . . . The trucks thumped heavily past, one by one, with a slow inevitable movement. . . . Then they curved away towards the coppice where the withered oak leaves dropped noiselessly. . . . In the open, smoke from the engine sank and cleaved to the rough grass. The fields were dreary and forsaken. Beyond them the pit-bank loomed up, flames liked red sores licking its ashy sides, in the afternoon's stagnant light.

Page 35—Question 1
Nowadays one does not dog-fight at all over the sky except on very rare occasions.

Punctuation

20 Parentheses, marked by commas, which improve sentences

A parenthesis is a word, or a group of words, that has been set aside from the main flow of a sentence by being enclosed between a pair of punctuation marks. The marks may be a pair of commas, or a pair of dashes, or a pair of brackets. We use commas for this purpose very often. They set the words aside in the lightest possible way:

> A stranger, perhaps, would not have noticed it.

> Her mother, she knew, would be beginning to worry.

The secret, often, of giving a sentence a shape or a rhythm, is to have a parenthesis in it. Here are two ways of punctuating the same piece of writing:

> We have to resign ourselves to the fact that the answer to this question and probably to many others too lies sealed up forever in Shakespeare's tomb at Stratford.

> We have to resign ourselves to the fact that the answer to this question, and probably to many others too, lies sealed up forever in Shakespeare's tomb at Stratford.

Making that middle phrase a parenthesis turns a shapeless sentence into a balanced one. Here is another shapeless sentence:

> It seems that among the documents that have been found is a letter that proves him to be completely innocent of the charges that have been laid against him.

That sentence, unlike the previous one, has no hidden parenthesis in it round which commas could go. So we will re-arrange the order of the words in such a way as to give it one:

> Among the documents that have been found, it seems, is a letter that proves him to be completely innocent of the charges that have been laid against him.

44

1   In each of the following sentences two of the commas that the author put in, to form a parenthesis, could have been left out; and in the version given here they have been. Will you write out the sentences, putting back into each one the two missing commas. Notice, in each case, the improvement that is brought about in the shape and balance of the sentence. The quotations all come from *Treasure Island*, by Stevenson:

He was hunched as if with age or weakness and he wore a huge old tattered sea-cloak with a hood.

It was a bitter cold winter with hard frosts and heavy gales and it was plain from the first that my poor father was unlikely to see the spring.

Right in front of me not half a mile away I beheld the Hispaniola under sail.

I had quite made up my mind that the mutineers after their repulse that morning had nothing nearer their hearts than to up anchor and away to sea.

2   The sentences in the next group have been altered in a different way. What Stevenson had as a parenthesis— coming during the course of the sentence, and enclosed between a pair of commas—has been taken out from there and put at the beginning. Will you rewrite each sentence as he wrote it. But first, here is an example. *The altered version*: 'Therefore it was plain that the attack would be developed from the north.' *What Stevenson wrote*: 'It was plain, therefore, that the attack would be developed from the north.'

As you may fancy, I was very uneasy and alarmed and it rather added to my fears to observe that the stranger was certainly frightened himself.

For his part the captain stood staring at the signboard like a bewildered man.

I think it went sorely with all of us to leave those men there in that wretched state.

21 Parentheses, marked by commas, which spoil sentences

These minor characters add a touch of humour to, and relieve the sadness of, the play.

The two commas wrench that sentence into a most unnatural shape. It was quite unnecessary:

These minor characters add a touch of humour to the play and relieve the sadness of it.

Here is another disrupted sentence, with the parenthesis wedged into the middle of the verb:

These ancient tombs have never been, and probably never will be, found.

These ancient tombs have never been found and probably never will be.

A jolt will always be liable to occur if a parenthesis is inserted immediately after a word that has a strong urge to lead straight on:

He is one of those people who, no matter what arguments are put to them, will never alter their views.

That is a stilted way of writing. No doubt there are times when for some reason or other it is necessary to compose a sentence in that way. But some writers do it when there is no need to. They seem to enjoy it. It would have been easy to have arranged that last sentence naturally:

He is one of those people who will never alter their views, no matter what arguments are put to them.

1   Rearrange these sentences (in the same way as we rearranged those on the opposite page) so as to get rid of the awkward parentheses that disrupt them:

This way of tackling the job introduces more pleasure into, and relieves the monotony of, the work.

He should have, and on one occasion nearly did, become Prime Minister.

They decided to take the longer, rather than the quicker but more dangerous, route.

Although this story could be, and often has been, told at length, we can only summarize it here.

We were to return to camp at once, we were told, if, when we applied for permission to cross the border, we detected any sign of hostility on the part of the guards, however slight.

2   Here is a sentence from *Washington Square*, by Henry James:

He had married, at the age of twenty-seven, for love, a very charming girl, Miss Catherine Harrington, of New York, who, in addition to her charms, had brought him a solid dowry.

Will you rewrite it in such a way that the language has some chance to flow, even if only for a little distance, instead of being so unnaturally constricted by all those parentheses. (But don't eliminate any that are necessary: 'for love', for example, derives a special emphasis from being enclosed between commas.)

22　Semicolons and colons

What is the difference?

A semicolon is simply a mild version of a full stop. It marks the end of a sentence, as a full stop does, but it does not do it so emphatically:

> The garden was badly neglected. The paths were choked with moss and weeds; dandelions and thistles stood amidst tufts of straggling grass; the vine had pulled down the trellis and lay sprawled over the flagstones.

A colon, too, marks the end of a sentence, but it also conveys a piece of information. It tells the reader that in the next sentence the writer is going to explain what he has just said:

> The house had two great advantages: it was cheap, and it was near London.

> This book is more than just another crime novel: it is a study of American society in the 1920s.

> The reason why she kept belittling her husband was quite obvious: she was jealous of his success.

> He had only one fault: he was inclined to fuss over unimportant details.

> We soon saw where the sound was coming from: a small bird had got caught in the netting.

Colons are very useful. There are certain intonations of the voice that we could never capture in writing if we did not have them to help us. But we could manage quite easily without semicolons. On most occasions a full stop will do just as well.

1   Each of the following passages consists of two sentences, with a line between them instead of a punctuation mark. Write out each passage, putting either a semicolon or a colon in place of the line. Four of the passages need semicolons (because in those there is just a simple pause after the first sentence), and four need colons (because in those the second sentence is an explanation of what is said in the first one):

We guessed at once why she had moved away from the district___ she had found life too lonely there.

He sat on the edge of the chair, and his hands trembled slightly___ he looked older and more frail, I thought.

Towards evening a pair of swans flew over the lake___ we could hear the distant swish of their wings.

The message he sent back was uncompromisingly blunt___ we were to return to camp immediately.

The site had another disadvantage___ it was low-lying and liable to be flooded in winter.

At first there was no response to my knock___ then a light appeared through a crack in the door and I heard the shuffle of footsteps.

It was a dry, windless night___ the only sound was the distant rumble of traffic on the by-pass.

The explanation he gave us was not convincing___ it was too slick.

2   Will you now write a short passage, consisting of some three or four sentences, in which you use at least one semicolon. Choose any subject you like, but not anything that is mentioned in the examples given in this book. Here is one suggestion: write a brief description of an indoor scene.

3   Now write a passage consisting of only two sentences, in such a way that you need to use a colon after the first one. Here are a few suggestions for the subject-matter: an event spoilt by bad weather . . . somebody's appearance or character or behaviour . . . losing the way.

23　Single dashes—pointing forward

We use a dash when we want to direct the reader's attention forward to some word or phrase which we have saved up for the end of our sentence:

He loved only one person—himself.

The house was everything we had hoped it would be—old, rambling, and full of character.

Then, from far down in the valley, came the sound he had dreaded hearing—the crashing of trees as the flood-water swept through.

A comma would not do in those sentences. It would look weak and wrong, because it would not give them the forward impetus they need.

1   In four of the following sentences a dash is needed, and the comma that has been used instead does not make the meaning so clear. Decide which those four are, and then write them out with the dash put in:

We were determined to make up the time we had lost,   _
even if it meant travelling through the night.

She told him of these events in a casual, off-hand manner, as though such matters were too trivial even to mention.

In the drawer we found a miscellany of old coins,   _
florins, farthings, half-crowns, and a guinea piece.

It turned out to be just such a morning as she had hoped it would be, hot, sunny, and yet with a touch of autumn freshness in the air.

He undertook with the utmost willingness every task he was given, no matter how mean or petty it was.   _

Then, faintly, from beyond the curve in the road, we heard another sound, the tramp of soldiers on the march.   _

I could recall, vividly, every detail, the rain, the fading light, the look of sadness on his face.   _

2   In this next passage three of the commas are wrong: one should be a colon, one a dash, and one a full stop (but not in that order). Will you write the passage out, with these mistakes put right:

It took them nearly an hour to search the library, but it was a waste of effort for they found nothing. They went back into the hall, the last of the daylight had nearly gone. Only one room remained to be searched, the boxroom on the first floor. They crept up the stairs, which were now shrouded in darkness. But when they came to the little door at the top they found themselves face to face with one more unexpected difficulty, the knob of the door-handle had been pulled off and it was impossible to turn the latch.

24　Single dashes—afterthoughts

Single dashes have another use, quite different from the one we have just been looking at. They are useful when we want to show that something is being added as an afterthought:

> These new documents will greatly increase our knowledge of this period of history—if they are genuine.

Only a dash can suggest the meaningful pause the speaker made there, and the tone of voice he used. A comma would not do, because it would make the sentence seem all of one piece. Here are two more examples:

> They completed the voyage in less than six hours—or so they told us.

> It should turn out to be a very useful invention indeed —provided it works.

Sometimes the added part takes the form of a comment on what has been said:

> Tom Stoppard has managed to compress these events into less than ten minutes' acting time—a wonderful feat of craftsmanship.

> At this point the river begins to flow very swiftly—too swiftly for anyone who is not a highly skilled canoeist.

And sometimes it takes the form of an explanation:

> After a few hours they reached the eastern shore of the lake—the shore, that is, which forms part of the Swiss border.

1   In three of the following sentences a dash should have been used, and the comma that has been used instead is either wrong or not so effective. Write out those three, punctuating them with dashes:

The first day's march was a dreadful ordeal, even for those of us who were used to long marches.

We found nothing in the cave, nothing, that is, except the odd bits of wood and rubbish that the tide always leaves behind.

The words of the song are sad too, even sadder, in some ways, than the music.

They decided to swim across, a very risky undertaking at that time of year.

The northern slopes were thickly wooded, mostly with pine and birch.

2   Make up a sentence which ends with an afterthought and which needs a dash to indicate this. Choose your own subject-matter. Here is one suggestion: make some statement or other, but then have second thoughts and express a doubt about the truth of it.

3   Now make up a sentence which ends with an explanation of what is said in the main part of it, and which needs a dash to show that the explanation was added as an afterthought. You can include the words 'that is' in the last part if you want to.

4   He wanted to leave, he said, as soon as possible.
    He wanted to leave, he said—as soon as possible.

The first of those sentences can be an answer either to this question: 'Do you want to leave or stay?'—or to this one: 'Do you want to leave now or later?' But the second sentence can be an answer to only one of those two questions. To which one? And why?

25 Single dashes—gathering up the thread of a sentence

Occasionally the opening part of a sentence may take the form of quite a long list. Suppose we want to say what the qualities of a great explorer are. We begin:

> Clear-headedness, courage, cheerfulness, a willingness to sacrifice oneself for others, and, above all, exceptional powers of physical endurance. . . .

By now we have gone on for so long that we need to take a new breath, as it were, and start again. So we put a dash, to mark a pause, and then continue with a 'pick-up' word—like *this* or *that* or *these*—which will gather up into itself the whole of the list:

> Clear-headedness, courage, cheerfulness, a willingness to sacrifice oneself for others, and, above all, exceptional powers of physical endurance—these are the qualities we expect to find in a great explorer.

Usually, as in that sentence, the pick-up word comes immediately after the dash. But it doesn't always. In this sentence, for example, it is the last word of all:

> A treacherous surface, continual blizzards, a thin atmosphere of intense cold—no expedition that has ever been mounted could have survived conditions like those.

1   Make up a sentence in which the opening part consists of a list that needs to be followed by a dash.

2   In this next passage one of the commas should have been a dash, one a full stop, and one a colon (but not in that order). Will you write the passage out, with these mistakes put right:

It was a bleak January morning, I leant on the parapet and stared across the river towards Westminster. Heaps of yellowed snow covered the pavements, and a veil of fog hung in the air. The scene was unspeakably dreary, drearier, I felt, than anything I had ever contemplated before. After a few moments it occurred to me that everything was strangely quiet, and I realised why, the bridge, and all the routes round Parliament Square, were closed to traffic.

3   Here is another passage in which some of the commas are wrong. One should have been a colon, one a full stop (or possibly a semicolon), and one a dash. Rewrite the passage with these mistakes put right:

He made his way along the valley for about a mile, walking slowly and casually so as not to arouse suspicion, then he turned aside and entered the woods. He pushed quickly through the undergrowth, and after a few minutes he came to the edge of the moor, the northern edge, that is, not far from Didford. He began to race across the open ground, but before he had gone far he realised that he had made one serious miscalculation, he had underestimated the length of time it would take for the mist to clear.

26 Dashes used in pairs to mark a parenthesis

Dashes shut a parenthesis away more sharply than commas do. We use them when the words we are slipping in, in the middle of our sentence, are not really part of it at all:

My favourite book—I must have read it four or five times at least—is *Wuthering Heights.*

In view of his lack of experience—it was his first time on stage, we must remember, as a professional actor—he gave a very good performance indeed.

Commas would not have worked in those sentences: the reader would have lost his way. Brackets would have done. But perhaps dashes look better. Perhaps they lead the reader along more smoothly.

1   All the following sentences contain parentheses, enclosed by commas. But in three of them the commas do not mark off the parenthesis sharply enough, and the reader is liable to get muddled: a pair of dashes is needed. Write out those three sentences, putting dashes instead of commas:

From where we were sitting, we had paid the top price and were only two rows from the front, we could see every shade of expression on the actors' faces.

He read this book as a boy, long before he began writing novels himself, and yet its influence can be felt in all his books, even in those he wrote when he was over sixty.

The Dutchman stood his ground while the Italian, a much lighter and nimbler fellow, danced round him making feints and jabs.

This ancient manuscript, it is even older, according to some scholars, than the Dead Sea Scrolls, has been interpreted in different ways.

Only part of the blame, it now seems, and not the whole of it, as was at first supposed, should be laid on the ship's captain.

These bouts of depression, which were becoming more and more prolonged, he remained sunk in them, sometimes, for days on end, were beginning to spoil the life of the whole family.

2   Make up three sentences (not connected with each other) in such a way that each one could serve as an example of how dashes can be used to enclose a parenthesis. Write them about anything you like, but not anything mentioned on these pages. Here are a few suggestions: an outdoor sport . . . an airport . . . an elderly person . . . the sea . . . a royal visit . . . a garden.

Imagery

27 Imagery and similes

Imagery comes into a person's writing whenever he compares one thing to another in an imaginative way.

The moon looked like a silver coin.

That is imagery.

There are different kinds. That kind is a simile. It is a simile because the writer makes the comparison in a straightforward manner: he just says, quite openly, that the one thing looked like the other one. Here is another way of forming a simile:

The moon was sailing through the clouds as swiftly and smoothly as a ship.

That, too, is a straightforward comparison.

When a writer uses a simile his imagination never overwhelms the reality. 'The moon looked like a silver coin'. The person who wrote that did not suppose, even for a moment, that the moon *was* a silver coin. A simile rules out an imaginative leap of that kind. If you think the moon is *like* a silver coin, you cannot think it *is* one.

1   Do you think that any of the similes in the following pieces of writing are poor in any way? (Sentimental, perhaps? Or ridiculous? Or too obvious? Or inappropriate?) It might be thought that two or three are— possibly four. If you think any are, indicate which by writing down the first two or three words of the extract; and then briefly explain why you think so.

The names of the authors are given on page 72. But do not look until you have done the question.

The drive twisted and turned like an enchanted ribbon through the dark and silent woods.

She primmed up her mouth tighter and tighter, puckering it as if it were sewed.

The timbered cottage, with its sloping, cloak-like roof, was old and forgotten.

He pulled her close against him and his lips came down on hers. It was a feeling so perfect that it was as if she kissed the sunlight.

The keyboard of the piano looked like a mouthful of bad teeth, chipped, yellow, and some missing altogether.

He looked at the sky and saw the white cumulus built like friendly piles of ice cream.

Before them, but some distance off, there stood a green hill-top, treeless, rising like a bald head out of the encircling wood.

2   Now write a short paragraph in which you describe a night scene (a floodlit stadium? . . . a coffee bar? . . . a city scene at night, perhaps by a river? . . .). Introduce one simile.

28 Metaphors

> The moon was a ghostly galleon, tossed upon cloudy seas.

That is not a simile. The writer did not say that the moon was *like* a ghostly galleon: he allowed his imagination to carry him further than that. To him, as he wrote that sentence—for we must take him at his word—the moon *was* a ghostly galleon. When a writer declares, in that way, that two different things are one and the same, instead of just saying that they are like each other, he is using a metaphor.

The writer *mentioned* the moon, in that metaphor. So the idea of it, as a reality, was present at the back of his mind. It is possible to go further, and not mention it at all:

> I looked up and saw that the silver ship of the night was already sailing the sky.

There, the writer's imagination took him still further away from reality. For a brief moment, while the spell lasted, the moon ceased to exist, and he saw only a silver ship. His vision, as he wrote those words, was so completely dominated by his imagination that the image overwhelmed the reality and put it out of his mind, so that he did not even mention it. A metaphor like that one is the very opposite of a simile. In a simile it is the reality that predominates.

1   Here are four descriptions of the earth, seen from the
air. In the first two it is seen during the daytime; in the
last two, at night:

He was about a thousand feet up, and he looked down
and saw flat green country with fields and hedges and
no trees. He could see some cows in the field below
him. (Roald Dahl: *Over to You*)

Bond had a moment of exhilaration as the sun came up.
Twenty thousand feet below, the houses began to show
like grains of sugar spilt across a brown carpet. Nothing
moved on the earth's surface except a thin worm of
smoke from a train, the straight white feather of a
fishing boat's wake across an inlet, and the glint of
chromium from a toy motor car caught in the sun. (Ian
Fleming: *Diamonds are Forever*)

A moment later they were flying only fifty feet above the
roof-tops of the town. They could spot scattered lights
below them, as the black-out was anything but perfect.
The glow from the snow, which was broken by black
patches, enabled them to pick out the principal
buildings. (Dennis Wheatley: *Faked Passports*)

The first lights showed below us—long ribbons of
amber, orange, white and blue. And then the great
sprawling mass of the city seen only as slashes of
arterial brilliance, the blank spaces in between dotted
with the pinpoints of individual street lights like
thousands upon thousands of tiny perforations in a
black sheet of paper. (Hammond Innes: *The Strode
Venturer*)

A skilful use of imagery forms the very essence of good
descriptive writing. Of those four passages, two are
enriched by it and two are not. As an experiment will you
rewrite the two that are merely factual in such a way as to
introduce some imagery into them. Do not add very
much. Just a few touches will make all the difference.

2   Now write two descriptions of your own of an aerial
view—one seen in the daytime, the other at night.

29 *Of* metaphors; metaphors that reside in the verb; personification

There are other ways of forming metaphors, as well as those we have looked at. We can use an *of* to link the image with the reality:

A sea of corn. . . . A pillar of smoke. . . . A jewel of a day . . . a giant fist of rock.

Or we can put the image into the verb. This is a very neat and economical way:

The car sped along the road. . . . The car rocketed along the road. The wind was blowing the dead leaves into a heap. . . . The wind was whipping the dead leaves into a heap. A flash of lightning lit the sky. . . . A flash of lightning tore a crevice in the sky.

Sometimes, when you use a metaphor, you may find that you are at the same time introducing a personification. A personification is simply a metaphor which suggests that the object is a living being:

The moon smiled down. . . . The turbo-jets screamed. . . . The sea was angry.

In that last example, you will notice, the metaphor resides in the adjective.

1   Will you make each of the following sentences metaphorical by changing the verb, in the same way as we did in those three examples on the opposite page. You can either put one word in place of it (as we did in the first two examples), or a group of words (as we did in the third one). You may find that your metaphor often takes the form of a personification. Try to be original and to avoid clichés:

The exhaust *emitted* black smoke.

The rain *fell* on the hard, smooth leaves of the holly-tree.

The pneumatic drill *bored* through the slab of concrete.

A violent wind *blew* through the empty barn.

He put a fresh log on the fire and watched as a thin yellow flame began to *encircle* it.

The long line of cars *moved* slowly down the twisting mountain road.

2   Here is a difficult task. The following passages come from books by Ian Fleming. In each passage one of the metaphorical verbs that he used has been replaced by a literal one. The replacements are in italics. Will you suggest metaphorical verbs that would go well in those contexts. When you have made your suggestions turn to page 72 to see what he wrote:

The heavy stone came down. The broken scorpion *twitched* in its death agony.

The slot machines were right in his path. He gave them all a try, and once two cherries and a bell-fruit *ejected* back three coins for the one he played.

The sweat began to *appear* on Bond's forehead.

Bond set off up the steep slope of the tunnel. Clusters of bats hung like bunches of withered grapes from the roof, and when, from time to time, his head brushed against them they *scattered* twittering into the darkness.

30   Sustained metaphors

Sometimes, in a descriptive passage, a writer will sustain just one metaphor through several sentences. He will explore it and elaborate it, in such a way as to find in it more and more resemblances to what he is describing— almost (so one feels sometimes) as though he had challenged himself to find as many as possible.

In this passage, which comes from *Lord of the Flies*, William Golding explores the similarities between a fire on a mountainside and a devouring animal. The fire is just starting:

> Small flames stirred at the bole of a tree and crawled away through leaves and brushwood, dividing and increasing. One patch touched a tree trunk and scrambled up like a bright squirrel. The smoke increased, sifted, rolled outwards. The squirrel leapt on the wings of the wind and clung to another standing tree, eating downwards. Beneath the dark canopy of leaves and smoke the fire laid hold on the forest and began to gnaw. Acres of black and yellow smoke rolled steadily towards the sea. At the sight of the flames the boys broke into shrill, excited cheering. The flames crept as a jaguar creeps on its belly towards a line of birch-like saplings.

Will you now write a descriptive passage, of about the same length as the extract on the opposite page, based on a single sustained image. Choose whatever subject-matter and whatever image you like; but if you want some suggestions here are three.

Describe the view from a boat in a rough sea, and let your description be dominated by an image of mountains. In other words, interpret the sea as a mountainous scene, with lofty peaks, precipitous slopes, snow-caps, avalanches, and so on. Or describe a wood in terms of a cathedral—from the point of view, perhaps, of someone walking through it. Or describe a foggy city street as though it were an underwater scene—again, perhaps, from the point of view of someone walking along it or driving along it.

Do not make *all* the sentences in your description metaphorical. That would overload it badly. Let some of them be factual, as a contrast. And you can, if you want to, include similes (William Golding, you will notice, includes two).

31 Dead metaphors

A dead metaphor is one that has been used so often that the picture it once conjured up has been worn away:

He barged into the room. . . . A ray of hope. . . . To see something in a new light. . . . He was dogged by bad luck. . . . The crux of the matter. . . . To undermine a person's confidence. . . . To ride roughshod over other people's feelings. . . . On the brink of war. . . . He avoided the usual pitfalls. . . .

—in just those few expressions there is a wealth of pictorial imagery, but constant use has obliterated it all.

The language is full of dead metaphors. There is nothing wrong with them. Many of them have become the accepted way of saying something. But now, because their pictures have faded, it seems that all they are doing is making a literal statement.

1   Make up four sentences, and let each one contain a dead metaphor connected with either an animal or a bird. There is one example on the opposite page. Here is one more: 'He craned his neck out of the window.'

2   Now write down three expressions, and let each one contain a dead metaphor in which a feature of the landscape is associated with a part of the body. Here is an example: 'the mouth of the river'.

3   Here is an extract from *Sons and Lovers*, by D. H. Lawrence:

> The sun was going down. The hills of Derbyshire were blazed over with red sunset. Mrs Morel watched the sun sink from the glistening sky, leaving a soft flower-blue overhead, while the western space went red, as if all the fire had swum down there, leaving the bell cast flawless blue. The mountain-ash berries across the field stood fierily out from the dark leaves. A few shocks of corn in a corner stood up as if alive; she imagined them bowing. In the east a mirrored sunset floated pink opposite the west's scarlet. Now and again, a swallow cut close to her.

'. . . leaving the bell cast flawless blue.' Explain why this is a metaphor and not a simile. Can you re-word it in such a way as to turn it into a simile?

4   Here are some of the verbs Lawrence uses: '. . . blazed . . . swum . . . bowing . . . floated . . . cut'. Will you write them down, and after each one put either an 'L', if the verb is used in its literal sense, or an 'M', if it is used metaphorically. Be careful over 'bowing'.

32   Mixed metaphors

Here is one:

> I had sunk into a deep morass of despair, and although my friends tried to comfort me I could see no light at the end of the tunnel.

They can be very funny. The humour does not just lie in their absurdity: it lies also in the fact that the writer or speaker remains comically unaware that he has said anything funny at all:

> That argument was a complete red herring, and I am surprised that you swallowed it.

The mixed metaphors that one comes across in writing are not likely to be as blundering as that. A writer is not going to be so stupid as to bundle together, in an obvious way, two incompatible images. But there is another trap, which it is easier to fall into—the mistake of setting up one image and then making it do something it cannot do:

> Suddenly, with a loud huzza, a little cloud of pirates leapt from the woods on the north side, and ran straight for the stockade. (From *Treasure Island*, by R. L. Stevenson)

Stevenson's little cloud has not only to jump and run, but also to give out a cheer. Barbara Cartland made the same kind of mistake when she wrote this sentence (in *Bride to the King*):

> It was a room, she thought, that might have stepped straight out of a fairy-story.

A room with legs?

1   Rewrite the following sentences in such a way as to
'unmix' the metaphors. In each sentence there are two
metaphors that do not go together. Either change one so
that it conforms with the other; or else replace one of
them with a literal statement. Here is an example. Consider the sentence that is quoted at the beginning of the
opposite page. We could write: 'I had entered a dark
tunnel of despair, and although my friends tried to
comfort me I could see no light at the end of it'. Or: 'I
had sunk into a deep morass of despair, and although my
friends tried to comfort me I felt that I would never cease
to be miserable':

The shadow of a smile lit up his face.

In those days many people felt that they were standing
on the threshold of a new chapter in human history.

There was a searchlight battery on the headland, and
long pencils of light towered up through the darkness.

It was his aim to keep this skeleton-in-the-cupboard
concealed from everyone, but before long his neighbours
began to get wind of it.

Heavy clouds began to blow across our path, and soon
we were bathed in a wall of mist.

He extended the hand of friendship to these people, but
all they did was throw it back in his face.

A gulf divided the two factions, and there seemed to be
no way of overcoming it.

This poisonous remark wounded her deeply.

2   Now make up three sentences (not connected with
each other) that could stand as examples of mixed metaphors. Do not make the blunders too unlikely: let them
be such that one could believe that someone might have
made them.

Answers and correct versions of quoted extracts

Page 37—Question 1
Macalister's boy took one of the fish and cut a square out of its side to bait his hook with. The mutilated body (it was alive still) was thrown back into the sea.

In the morning they buried Mrs Collard. The serjeant gòt a coolie, and he dug a shallow grave. They lowered her into it covered with a blanket, and Mrs Horsefall read a little out of the Prayer Book. Then they took away the blanket because they could not spare that, and the earth was filled in.

Page 61—Question 1
Daphne du Maurier: *Rebecca*. D. H. Lawrence: *The Fox*. D. H. Lawrence: *England, my England*. Barbara Cartland: *The Dream and the Glory*. Leslie Thomas: *This Time Next Week*. Ernest Hemingway: *The Old Man and the Sea*. J. R. R. Tolkien: *The Fellowship of the Ring*.

Page 65—Question 2
The broken scorpion whipped in its death agony. . . . once two cherries and a bell-fruit coughed back three coins. . . . the sweat began to bead on Bond's forehead. . . . they exploded twittering into the darkness.

Presenting an argument

33 For and against

When you are putting forward an argument in favour of
some point of view, you may want to mention the
objections that can be raised against it, so that you can
dismiss them. It is usually best to mention them first: then
you can end up by affirming the rightness of the point of
view you favour. What is *not* a good thing to do is to
dodge about from one side of the argument to the other:

> The television film of *David Copperfield* was a fine
> production, but the fact remains that seeing the film of
> a classic is no substitute for reading the book, but the
> film must have given many people who would never
> read Dickens some idea of what his writing is like.

In that passage the first 'but' turns the reader's thoughts
away from the line they were following, and a moment
later a second one turns them back to it. The second one
will disappear if we arrange the ideas more logically, and
deal first with the two points that stand against the view
we are putting forward:

> The television film of *David Copperfield* was a fine
> production, and it must have given many people who
> would never read Dickens some idea of what his writing
> is like. But the fact remains that seeing the film of a
> classic is no substitute for reading the book.

1   Will you now improve this passage, which has the same kind of fault—a double switch—as the passage on the opposite page:

I prefer to do my shopping in small shops rather than in a big department store, although in a big store it is possible to buy everything under one roof, which is an advantage, because in small shops they give you a personal service.

Begin 'It is true that . . .', and deal with the big store first (the 'against' side) before you mention the small shops. Doing that will make the passage clearer and also get rid of some unnecessary repetition.

2   Now improve these passages. Again, each one has the same kind of fault as the passage on the opposite page:

Lord of the Flies is a study of human nature, but on the surface it might seem to be nothing more than a book about violence and cruelty, but at a deeper level it is a study of the different ways in which people might behave if they were freed from social restrictions.

I believe that a God of some kind must exist, but I do not believe in the conventional God-the-father figure, because it seems to me that there is no other way of explaining life.

On the whole, I think, television commercials are harmful, although it is true that the revenue from them goes to sponsor some worthwhile programmes that would not otherwise be shown, because they encourage greed, and the style of some of them is cheap and degrading. (Make two sentences of this passage.)

3   Write a short paragraph, of three or four sentences, in which you put forward an argument either for or against this proposal: that one is likely to gain less from seeing a film or television adaptation of a novel than from reading the novel.

Include in your argument at least one point that could be raised against the view you support, and deal with this first, before you explain your own view.

34   Stage by stage

It is nearly always best, if you have a passage of close
reasoning to unfold, to divide it into stages and have a
separate sentence for each stage. People sometimes pour
out, in one go, quite long stretches of argument—probably
because it all came into their minds at once and they felt
they had to get it down quickly, before it slipped away:

> In my opinion those people who blame the violence of
> modern society on the bad influence of television and
> say that the violent scenes in television films encourage
> violence in real life are wrong, because art is a reflec-
> tion of life and those films only reflect an attitude that
> already exists and are not the cause of it.

It is a good idea to write it down like that, but it will only
be a rough draft. The writer should look at it again and
try to improve it by dividing it up, so that the argument
will be unfolded step by step:

> Some people blame the violence of modern society on
> the bad influence of television. The violent scenes in
> television films, they say, encourage violence in real
> life. In my opinion they are wrong. For art is a reflection
> of life, and those films only reflect an attitude that
> already exists. They are not the cause of it.

1 'Divide your argument into stages, and have a separate sentence for each stage.' That piece of advice might well be recommended to anyone who writes like this:

The fact that Hyde, the doctor's stunted evil self, manifests his evil in acts of physical brutality rather than in, say, sexual licence, although the moral defectiveness to which he owed his release relates to the kind of hedonistic adventurism that Stevenson himself practised in his bohemian days, is perhaps evidence of Stevenson's instinctive awareness of the relation between sensuality and sadism, but it is more likely to result from the impossibility in the 1880's of describing acts of violent sensuality with the frankness they require if they are to administer to the reader the kind of shock which the story demands. (From *Robert Louis Stevenson and his World*, by David Daiches.)

It would not be fair to ask you to sort out a muddle like that. Instead will you express, in two sentences, the main point the writer is trying to make. The first instalment of it comes in the first three lines, the second one in the last five. In your version use your own words as much as you want to. For example, it might be a good idea to begin your second sentence like this: 'Stevenson probably wrote the story in this way because . . .'

2   Will you now improve this passage by altering it in two ways. Rearrange the ideas in a more logical order, so that you deal with the 'against' side first, before mentioning what 'I' thinks; and divide the passage into four sentences (with the third one very short):

I disagree with the view of some people who want to put a stop to the exploration of space and consider that it is too costly and maintain that the money would be better spent on such undertakings as medical research or the relief of poverty, because the exploration of space is an outlet for man's spirit of adventure, and life would not be worth living, in my opinion, if this spirit were stifled.

35 *But, also,* and a few other words

Some people think it is wrong to begin a sentence with a *but*. How they ever get hold of that idea is hard to explain. *But* is an excellent word to begin sentences with, and writers are always beginning them with it, because they prefer a light little word like that to the more literary *nevertheless* or the more pompous *however*.

Also sometimes sounds awkward when it comes at the beginning of a sentence. 'Also it must be remembered that this is a new field of study.' Many people would prefer to write: 'It must also be remembered. . . .' *Moreover*, which means much the same as *also*, can always stand at the beginning: 'Moreover it must be remembered . . .'

'It is true that . . .' is a useful expression. It is a warning that the writer is about to put forward some point that tells against his own view, and that in a moment he is going to come out on his own side again. So whenever we see this expression in a piece of writing we know that before long we are going to come to a *but* or a *however* or a *nevertheless*.

1   In each of the following passages there is one sentence that has a word missing. Write this sentence out with the word filled in, choosing it from among those mentioned on the opposite page:

The Council have compiled a set of statistics to prove their case. _____ statistics, as everyone knows, can be made to prove almost anything.

So far, in spite of a vigorous campaign, they have failed to win approval for their scheme. There are signs, _____ , that the opposition to it is crumbling.

I think that there should be a law against conducting opinion polls during an election campaign. For they can be very misleading, and though most of them are responsibly conducted not all of them are. _____ , as enquiries have shown, they sometimes influence the way people vote.

2   Write a short paragraph, of three or four sentences, in which you either favour or condemn modern architecture, or a particular modern building or group of buildings you are familiar with. Begin by mentioning a point of view opposed to your own and introduce it by using the expression 'It is true that . . .'

3   Now improve this passage by altering it in two ways. Rearrange the ideas in a more logical order, so that you deal with the pro-abolition side first, before coming to 'my' opinion (which is anti-abolition); and at the same time divide the passage into either three or four sentences:

In my opinion it would be a serious mistake to abolish film censorship, although it is true that it can be regarded as an interference with the liberties of the individual, and some quite sincere people have tried to get it abolished on these grounds, because other things need protection as well as liberty, such as children, for example, who need to be protected from seeing the horrifying scenes that occur in some films.

36 Paragraphs

It is important to have clear paragraphs. The very sight of the spaces between them encourages a reader. On the other hand, a page without any, packed with words, makes the heart sink.

A writer should begin a new paragraph every time he comes to a new aspect of his subject. In the opening sentences of it he will do well to give his readers a strong clue as to what it is going to be about. He may even tell them directly. In this way he will put them in the right frame of mind to read on.

Here is a passage a student wrote about the sport of gliding. He has arranged his ideas so clearly and straightforwardly that it could be taken as a model paragraph:

> Gliding will never become a popular sport. By a popular sport I mean one that is practised—not just watched—by large numbers of people. There are two reasons. One is that it is extremely expensive. A modern glider is a complicated machine, with a full panel of instruments, a radio link, airbrakes, an oxygen supply, and several other devices. Only a rich person can afford to possess one. The other reason is that gliding is a sport with a strong element of loneliness and danger in it. Sports of this kind are always the preserve cf the few.

Notice, in particular, how well the opening sentence does its job. It provides the key to the subject-matter of the paragraph in the simplest possible way. There is no fuss— no boring rigmarole like 'We will now consider the question of why gliding will never . . .'

1   A simple question often makes a very good beginning to a paragraph. It sounds pleasant, and in a neat, direct way it tells the reader what the paragraph is going to be about. For example, here is the opening sentence of an article about education:

> We will first of all try to achieve an understanding as to what the purpose of education is.

It's a heavy beginning. By putting it in the form of a question we can lighten it:

> What is the purpose of education?

Now here are three paragraph openings—all of them very heavy-sounding. Will you lighten them by turning them into questions:

> We will now examine the question of whether or not there is life after death. (5 words)

> Whether these excursions have any educational value or whether they are just pleasure jaunts is the question that must next be considered. (12 words)

> We must now ask ourselves if this argument is justified or not. (4 words)

2   Now write a paragraph, of roughly the same length as that one on the opposite page, about one of these subjects: another kind of sport . . . music . . . the circus . . . the theatre . . . computers . . . or any other subject you like to choose.

Think of your paragraph as being an extract from a longer piece of writing, and confine yourself to just one aspect of the subject. Make sure, before you begin, that you have an exact idea of what that aspect is: if you do not, you will almost certainly spoil the paragraph.